# POETRY EMOTIONS

## Middlesex

### Edited by Lisa Adlaml

First published in Great Britain in 2016 by:

 Young**Writers**

Remus House
Coltsfoot Drive
Peterborough
PE2 9BF
Telephone: 01733 890066
Website: www.youngwriters.co.uk
All Rights Reserved
Book Design by Ashley Janson
© Copyright Contributors 2015
SB ISBN 978-1-78624-012-5

Printed and bound in the UK by BookPrintingUK
Website: www.bookprintinguk.com

# Foreword

Welcome, Reader!

For Young Writers' latest competition, *Poetry Emotions*, we gave school children nationwide the task of writing a poem all about emotions, and they rose to the challenge magnificently!

Pupils could either write about emotions they've felt themselves or create a character to represent an emotion. Which one they chose was entirely up them. Our aspiring poets have also developed their creative skills along the way, getting to grips with poetic techniques such as rhyme, simile and alliteration to bring their thoughts to life. The result is this entertaining collection that allows us a fascinating glimpse into the minds of the next generation, giving us an insight into their innermost feelings. It also makes a great keepsake for years to come.

Here at Young Writers our aim is to encourage creativity in children and to inspire a love of the written word, so it's great to get such an amazing response, with some absolutely fantastic poems. This made it a tough challenge to pick the winners, so well done to *Olivia Hnat* who has been chosen as the best author in this anthology.

I'd like to congratulate all the young authors in *Poetry Emotions - Middlesex* - I hope this inspires them to continue with their creative writing.

Jenni Bannister
Editorial Manager

# Our charity partner for this academic year is ...

**YOUNGMINDS**

The voice for young people's **mental health and wellbeing**

**We're aiming to raise a huge £5,000 this academic year to help raise awareness for YoungMinds and the great work they do to support children and young people.**

If you would like to get involved visit
**www.justgiving.com/Young-Writers**

YoungMinds is the UK's leading charity committed to improving the emotional wellbeing and mental health of children and young people. They campaign, research and influence policy and practice on behalf of children and young people to improve care and services. They also provide expert knowledge to professionals, parents and young people through the Parents' Helpline, online resources, training and development, outreach work and publications. Their mission is to improve the emotional resilience of all children and to ensure that those who suffer ill mental health get fast and effective support.

**www.youngminds.org.uk**

# Contents

## The Smallberry Green
## Primary School, Isleworth

# The Poems

# Pride Is Everywhere

The sadness has passed,
As we roll down the emerald grass,
And the celebrations have begun,
After the test we had lots of fun,
We went to watch the shooting stars,
After that we looked for Mars,
Pride is everywhere,
And now I think that I can share,
I can hear the beautiful birds sing,
And glory now is about to begin,
God has helped me do these things,
Now I can pull the party popper strings.

**Stefania Belsito (10)**
Our Lady of the Visitation School, Greenford

# Untitled

I'm sitting on a bench with my parents
I can hear the birds singing,
The wind blowing and beautiful nature around me.
I can see the lime-green grass, the oak brown wood.
Although I'm always asking myself, is this life?

I'm sitting on a bench with my parents,
As happy as I can be,
Gazing around thanking God,
He made it such a beautiful place.

**Brajan Skiba (10)**
Our Lady of the Visitation School, Greenford

# The Best Day Ever

I am walking from school on a happy day.
I have celebrations after a roll down the hill.
I am happy.
I am so excited,
I am happy like I want to cheer,
Because it is my birthday.
After I want cake, nice chocolate cake full of marshmallows.

**Hannah Le-Roux (10)**
Our Lady of the Visitation School, Greenford

# The Anger Has Appeared

Deep in your body, there lies a cave, dark inside.
A monster called Anger has a slumber,
But when the tension gets too much, he appears,
Taking control over your thoughts and actions, bringing fear to others.
A volcano has appeared and erupted.
All my veins have burst and my eyes have popped.
I become a dark monster, willing to be violent.
I rage and transform into a demon.
The dark side has been activated and there is no stopping,
I will be a demon until Calm kicks in and leads me in the right
direction.

**Albert Gorges (10)**
Our Lady of the Visitation School, Greenford

# Happiness Is The Key

Happiness is something to cheer about,
Something to be happy about,
Not to be sad about,
You feel like you could do anything,
Happiness could be a smile without a face,
The wind whistled to everyone,
Which made them all happy,
There it is, some happiness,
You could feel great,
Nothing can stop you now,
Feel like a superhero,
I'm a superhero,
Joy and happiness are the same thing.

**Owen Stuart (10)**
Our Lady of the Visitation School, Greenford

# What Have I Done To Make You Do This?

Everywhere I go sadness follows me.
I feel like an unwanted banana tossed up in an old lunchbox.
I come to school with my head down trying not to get noticed.
Dreading the part of the day when I get made fun of.
I think to myself, *am I doing something wrong?*
I hope the day is not going to be long.
I don't know why they always choose me.
Is it because I am nice, pretty or dumb?
Anyway it is not much fun.
I'm bored of it, will it ever stop?
What will happen next, wait I'm in a shock.
What will I do to escape this now?
As the day goes on it gets even worse.
I will just have to wait and see what happens.

**Rosie Durkin (10)**
Our Lady of the Visitation School, Greenford

# Eww!

The sour feeling,
The horrible face.
Looking over your shoulder.
Knowing germs are a disgrace. *Eww!*

The bitter taste,
Your nose goo.
Never knowing when,
I will come out of you. *Eww!*

Don't read this on a full stomach,
If you are then quit.
But you probably won't listen,
Because you have gone to vomit! *Eww!*

You are lucky my friend
Now it is the end! *Blegh!*

**Noah Bello (10)**
Our Lady of the Visitation School, Greenford

7

# I Am Bored

My head is hanging down.
Sadly I'm wearing a frown.
My head in my hands.
While I'm dreaming of faraway lands.
I have nothing to do.
I really need the loo,
I can't be bothered to get up.
So I just yell what's up.
Finally I smile,
Luckily boredom goes away for a while.
Finally the bell rings.
I am free, yippee!

**Sadie Skinner (10)**
Our Lady of the Visitation School, Greenford

# Feeling Very Proud

With our hands in the air like we just do not care,
We strolled down the path and rolled down the grass.
Let the celebrations begin,
We promise we won't make a sin.
As I finally put down the books,
Now I can try out these looks.
Time to pull the party popper string,
And we can also try to sing.
I feel like Superwoman saving the world,
Time to get my hair curled.
And as I take my place,
I can now buy some lace.
I think I got a little obstinate!

**Nicole Yousif (10)**
Our Lady of the Visitation School, Greenford

# I Love My Life

I was thinking about something to do today,
Oh wait, it's my birthday tomorrow, hip hip hooray!
I went downstairs to the kitchen to make some food,
After I ate I went outside on the trampoline, that's good.
I went upstairs to the bedroom,
So I went to my album, looked around my pictures.
Downstairs my parents were doing fixtures.
My parents came to wake me up.
My friends were dancing around.
We ate some food, we had some fun,
Now it's time to play the drum,
It is now night, time to go to bed.

**Kasia Poelstepska (10)**
Our Lady of the Visitation School, Greenford

# The Day My Work Was Appreciated!

I was sitting in the classroom,
My friend was in the bathroom,
Miss Chapman came in,
She started to spin,
She called my name,
I thought it was a game.

I was sitting in the classroom,
My friend was in the bathroom,
She told me that I was chosen to meet an author in a different school,
I felt like jumping into a swimming pool.

The leaves were prancing around,
Then I fell to the ground,
It was heaven, I felt like I was in heaven.

**Oliwia Wisniowska (10)**
Our Lady of the Visitation School, Greenford

# Pride

P eople always practise goals to get better.
R ound the circle goes the ball, round and round goes the ball.
I was proud when I scored a goal!
'D on't shoot!' shouted Tom.
E veryone is different like brown skin, white skin or black skin.

**Agata Sowinska (9)**
Our Lady of the Visitation School, Greenford

# My First Ballet Exam

Oh no not again,
Ballet clothes back again.
I just hate this thing,
I say no, Mum says yes
Do I have to do exams? It might go wrong, it might go right.
Standing in front of a lady with a bun I'm so scared.
You wouldn't want to be in my skin.
Me standing there as red as a tomato feeling scared.

**Natalia Raczko (9)**
Our Lady of the Visitation School, Greenford

# Pride

P ride, I am with my holy community.
R ide a rainbow of pride.
I am filled with joy and pride,
D oubt, I am scared,
E veryone is proud.

**Victoria Pavlides (9)**
Our Lady of the Visitation School, Greenford

# Finally Here

The nine month wait is over, she is nearly born,
Sitting down on the sofa finally here.
Waiting five minutes, joy crawling around me finally here.
'She's born, she's born!' shouts my mum,
Tears of joy escapes my eyes,
Finally here, finally here.
I can't believe my heart but it's hard not to,
Nine months are over, nine months are over, finally here.

**Gio Haddad (10)**
Our Lady of the Visitation School, Greenford

# Untitled

Sending, sending your love never-ending,
Unconditional making all feel special,
Living life, loving all,
Loving all living life.

Bring us this gift,
This gift of love,
Send it to us,
As we shall send it to all,

All shall be shown love,
As we are shown,
Love is not a choice,
It is just there and not forced.

**Lavignia Magezi**
Our Lady of the Visitation School, Greenford

# Joy Is Great

Joy is peaceful, joy is sweet,
Where you may go it's joy you will meet.

Where there is joy there is happiness.
When people are cheering they show joy
When people laugh they are joyful.

Joy is fun, joy is great,
You are happy because of joy.

**Daniel Clarke**
Our Lady of the Visitation School, Greenford

# When I'm Free!

Once in the darkness,
I met a robot.
His name was Foxy,
And he wanted to torture me.

I closed my eyes,
And thought of freedom.
Foxy was scraping me
With claws I never see.

Now in the sunshine I'm flying free,
With an angel singing with me.
This is a feeling I'll never forget,
And the name of the feeling is going to be free!

**Filip Nowak (9)**
Our Lady of the Visitation School, Greenford

# Happiness

I like to be happy,
I do not like sad.
I like to be jolly everywhere around.
No one can stop me.
No one can go in front of me.
No one should say happiness is bad.
Hap, happy, happiness.
Hap, happy, happiness.

No one can be full of anger,
It's a very bad thing to be.
Happy, be happy.
Be full of happiness
It is spelt *h-a-p-p-i-n-e-s-s!*
Happiness is the best emotion of them all.

**Gabriella Ryan (9)**
Our Lady of the Visitation School, Greenford

# Excitement Party

I'm always excited at parties
It makes me look cool,
You can stay up all night plus,
Do whatever you want.

Don't bother about your parents.
Just have swag.
Show off to them like you don't care
Talk to people about what's on.

You wear gel everywhere,
Also be a kid who's an adult
Don't fear, excitement's here.
Be a bro hey yo.
It's as cool as a pro.

**Calum Taylor (9)**
Our Lady of the Visitation School, Greenford

# Joy Is The Best!

Joy is everywhere
You will find her anywhere.
There's a boy called Roy
And he has a lot of joy.
Don't fear, Joy is here!
Don't scream and shout
When Joy is about.
Turn that frown upside down.
Because . . . Joy is here!

**Chantal Mansour (9)**
Our Lady of the Visitation School, Greenford

# Happy

Happy is nice,
Happy is fun,
Happy is cool,
Happy is the best,
Happy is epic,
Happy is sick,
Happy is everyone,
Happy is people,
Happy is animals,
Happy is everything,
Happy is awesome.

**Marcus Micallef (9)**
Our Lady of the Visitation School, Greenford

# Happiness Is Important

It's great to smile,
Even if it's for a while.
It makes people have a big smile,
That you can even see from a mile.
It makes the world a better place,
Just from showing a smiley face.

Even if you're sad, just try to be grateful,
And think about the things that are beautiful.
Just please don't pull, please don't pull . . .
The face that is spelt *sad*.

It makes me feel angry and bad,
So remember be happy not . . . *sad*
It's easy to do and easy to show,
So just smile no matter what people do.

**Karolina Kawecka (10)**
Our Lady of the Visitation School, Greenford

# Pride

Pride is something that we all have.
We all see,
And we all keep.
Never stop, just begin on your knees.
You can do it, all you have to do is believe.
I have pride in me and I bet you do,
It's all over the world so,
Do what you have to do.
Nothing will stop me,
Because I've got it written
All over me.
Pride is something special, thank you.

**Sofie Marie Ramkalawan (9)**
Our Lady of the Visitation School, Greenford

# Joy

It's the opposite of sad.
It smells like summer.
It comes out laughter
And it feels like fun.

It runs in us
It is as happy as going to the seaside.
It makes you want to jump.
And it gives happiness to others.

It is the opposite of sad
It gives you friends
It gives a smile
Its name is joy!

**Rebecca Ishaya-Hana (10)**
Our Lady of the Visitation School, Greenford

# I'm Joy

Hello I'm Joy
I'm very joyful
How about you, are you joyful?
Have you met Mr Anger?
He is extremely rude,
Do you know him?

I'm on the school bus
We never fight, we're so quiet
That we are barely noticed!
Anger is here, hurry don't fear.
Because Joy is here and I'll sort it in a joyful way.

In my school
When I go there
They all shout and cheer when Joy is there.
When you have fear in you,
Don't worry take fear out of there and add joy in!

**Lewam Adenay (9)**
Our Lady of the Visitation School, Greenford

# Happy

Always be joyful,
Never let the anger out,
From underground,
It will be fun,
Just come with me,
We will be happy,
All day long,
Let's be together,
Put a smile on your face and be happy.
My friend, don't do the opposite of it.
It never shouts and it is so kind.
It does not even shout to the anger.

**Patrick Stepien (10)**
Our Lady of the Visitation School, Greenford

# Happiness

I love being happy with my friends,
I love it when people are happy.
I love it when people are friends,
I love it when I go on things I like.
I love it when everyone is happy.

I love it when I have things I like,
I love people when they are happy.
I love it when I go places with my family,
I love when I play with my friends and family,
I love it when Christmas comes.

**Millie Mulholland (10)**
Our Lady of the Visitation School, Greenford

# Happy Poem

**H** olidays are the best.
**A** ll the people love the beach,
**P** eople enjoy the hot summer,
**P** eople have fun when they win a medal,
**Y** ou would like the amazing summer.

**Elie (8)**
Our Lady of the Visitation School, Greenford

YoungWriters

# Happiness Is The Best Feeling You Can Have

H appiness means love and forgiveness
A ll in one big lovely family.
P atience is one of things God wants.
P ure happiness.
I s what God wants in our life.
N ice people are always blessed by God, but if you have been mean, God will forgive you.
E verything is beautiful in this universe.
S haring makes the world a better place.
S ome holidays are in a very holy place like Heaven or Croatia.

**Oludayo Ayomide Ogunberu (9)**
Our Lady of the Visitation School, Greenford

30

# Don't Be Scared

**S** ometimes I'm so tired,
**C** ome and help me,
**A** monster is coming,
**R** eally big monster,
**E** normous scary cake,
**D** amaged house is so scary.

**Martyna Michniak (8)**
Our Lady of the Visitation School, Greenford

# All About Love

Love is a beautiful feeling,
Each time you see that person your cheeks go red,
It's not an everyday emotion,
It's like a flower which grows and grows,
You will know it's him from the first time you see him,
He might even be your friend or someone you already know,
Sometimes love will come to you but sometimes you will have to come to it,
Now you will marry and then have a child,
Love is ended because of death but somewhere in the world it's still alive.

**Victoria Nawrocka (9)**
Our Lady of the Visitation School, Greenford

# Happiness Is . . .

**H** appiness is a joy in our lives,
**A** perfect day of playing with my friends,
**P** eace means love,
**P** resents being received on special occasions.
**I** love my holidays especially when I'm with my family and friends.
**N** othing gets in my way when I'm happy,
**E** verything is possible when I work as a team with my friends.
**S** ome things are mostly joyful in life.
**S** ometimes people are sad but we make them happy as well.

**Liliana Costa Alves (8)**
Our Lady of the Visitation School, Greenford

# When You're Happy

Happiness is all around,
Never be sad or I will be mad.
When you're happy jump for joy,
Put a lovely smile on your face.
Always be happy, never sad or you will make me sad too.
Being happy is as happy as being in love.
I love happy but not sad.
Have you ever been sad? I have.
But this poem has cheered me up.

**Ruby (8)**
Our Lady of the Visitation School, Greenford

# Sad And Silly

Sadness is sad and silly.
It makes people cry and go away.
When you are silly,
You are so sad because you get punished.
Think of the saddest time in your life,
Was it because you were silly or were you just sad?

**Hubert Truty (7)**
Our Lady of the Visitation School, Greenford

# You're Always Scared!

You're always scared when pots fall from nowhere.
The guy with a purple jumper, blue face and brown shoes
Comes out when you're scared.
Always be ready to be scared anywhere, any time, any day.
Get your revenge three . . . two . . . one . . . *Booooo!*

**Jaden Cumberbatch (7)**
Our Lady of the Visitation School, Greenford

# Joy Has Fun

Christmas is a very exciting day,
I hear people laughing and having a great time.
It's like something amazing is going to happen.
I can smell Christmas dinner *mmm, yum-yum!*
It's like I want to explode to bits!
*Pop, pop, whee, whee, yum!*
*Wow!*

**Alisha Edwards (7)**
Our Lady of the Visitation School, Greenford

# Christmas Day

Christmas is the best holiday ever.
Happiness comes when Christmas is near.
I like Christmas,
When the presents come I pop like a popped balloon.
I am happy like a dancing rainbow.
The most best thing about it is Santa,
Santa is like a friend giving presents.
Christmas comes, snow comes and plays with us.
Christmas always comes in December
And it comes with Santa happily, presents come for everyone.
At Christmas food is so delicious.

**Allan Maderazo (7)**
Our Lady of the Visitation School, Greenford

# I Am As Happy As A Christmas Tree

I am happy as a Christmas tree.
I love Christmas, I want to open my presents now!
Mummy, Daddy, call all those people.
Now make a lovely cake for me.
I love my cousins and family especially my sisters.
I love my godbrother and my godsister.
I want to eat the Christmas cake.
I will eat the icing.
Best day ever!

**Carmel Adenay (7)**
Our Lady of the Visitation School, Greenford

Young**Writers**

# Christmas

**C** hristmas is the best day ever!
**H** appy Santa should be happy every day.
**R** ed hat matches red clothes.
**I** really love Christmas
**S** anta is the best
**T** hing ever.
**M** erry Christmas Santa
**A** really fun day for everyone.
**S** anta will you come to me?

**Maja Gogolinska (7)**
Our Lady of the Visitation School, Greenford

# My Excited Birthday

My birthday felt exciting listening to the best fireworks.
How nice is it to be the birthday boy.
All of the presents are like a block of mountains.
The best part is when we play lots of birthday games.
My favourite game is musical statues.
*Best birthday boy.*

**Charbel Maroun**
Our Lady of the Visitation School, Greenford

# Joy From Christmas

When I was up again, Christmas was here once again.
I tiptoed to the front room and said, 'Wow!'
What a brilliant day.
I have been creating pictures of it,
It was shimmering like glitter, gleaming like snow, shimmering like a snowflake.

**Erin Judge (7)**
Our Lady of the Visitation School, Greenford

# Love

Roses are red,
Berries are blue,
If you love me,
I love you!

I'm the ruler
You're the highlighter,
I rule the world,
You make it brighter!

You light up the night
Because of your beautiful sight,
You make me sleep tight,
Because you make me feel you all right.

**Sahil Ral (10)**
Stanhope Primary School, Greenford

# Curious

There is a package on the table
Waiting just for you!
You're wondering who it's from
Maybe from your mum?

It's a triangular box
What could it be?
Is it actually for me?
You're drowning in curiosity.

Are you allowed?
Can you look?
Is there anyone behind you?
You don't know what to do!

Your heart is pounding like a drum
You are sinking in your skin
You cannot hold it anymore . . .
Curiosity gets the better of you . . .
*Rippp!*
*Huh!*

**Olivia Hnat (10)**
Stanhope Primary School, Greenford

# Sadness

Every day you feel sad,
People are bullying you.
People are calling you names
It feels like you want to cry every single day.

Sometimes you think you want to tell someone but you're too shy.
But when the bullies come you are really scared,
The only thing you do is just run away from them.

One day you think this is enough
You want this bullying to end forever
And be happy.

**Jarune Migilaite (10)**
Stanhope Primary School, Greenford

# Worry Monster

*Kta Bang*
I jumped in fear.
It made me cry
And I nearly died.

I opened my door
And there was blood on the floor.

Then the worry monster popped out
And I was never seen again.

**Abdulrahman Ali (10)**
Stanhope Primary School, Greenford

# The Beautiful Butterfly Of Hope

The beautiful butterfly of hope,
Slid through my window.
Glided in my room,
Making me bloom.

From all my worries now,
I think about the beautiful butterfly of hope.
Making me happy all my life,
Always stopping me when I cry,
I feel that no one can stop me now from being happy.
The beautiful butterfly of hope is by my side,
All the time.

When Pandora opened the box of spirits,
All the bad things came out of it.
But she was too upset to open it,
She was too upset to open it.
Then she realised that hope was there.

From that day on, everyone became happy, and hopeful!

**Vaideki Pramrajeenth (10)**
Stanhope Primary School, Greenford

# Curious

There was a basement in our house
There wasn't a doubt
That I shouldn't go in or out.

I heard a little growling sound
So I went down
Then I heard a scowl
I wondered what it could be
Maybe an owl.

Running down the stairs
I wondered if it was a bundle of bears
I went down there
It was a scare
I wondered what it was doing down there
It was a baby bear!

**Traveena Codling (10)**
Stanhope Primary School, Greenford

# Anger

I'm when you are not happy or allowed to join in.
I slowly get red like fire,
But when I pop I don't get calm,
I get bigger and bigger with not a care.
I am angry and I'm not very nice.

**Ryan Bradley (10)**
Stanhope Primary School, Greenford

# Happy Little Children

Happy little children,
Playing in the sun,
Running around like crazy.
And having lots of fun!

Happy little children,
Quickly skipping along,
One of them is singing,
A very tuneful song!

Happiness is spreading,
All around the world
Helping people become kind,
Including all the girls.

Happy, healthy children,
Having fun with their friends,
I was as happy as a horse,
And so are my friends!

And that is the poem of happiness,
And this is exactly how it ends!

**Kya Woolford (8)**
Stanhope Primary School, Greenford

# Anger

Anger hides in the deepest places,
Only comes out when I lose all the races!
Anger flares up in flames,
When I am left out of games.

I try to control it,
But I always get angry when they call me nitwit!
I feel steam boiling inside me,
I just want to quit!

My clenching fists as hard as rock,
I think I will chop a block.
I really want to miss school!
I will try to be cool.

If only I listened to Mum,
Instead of sucking my thumb!
If only I just listened.
I would have glistened!

**Nethmi Illagolla (8)**
Stanhope Primary School, Greenford

# Beautiful Love

The first time I saw her I fell in love with her beautiful eyes
And started dreaming about them.
After a week where I had been dreaming of the beautiful girl
I asked her for her phone number,
It made me feel so big and grown up for once.
The very day I looked at her beautiful self on What's App it was so wonderful.
In the meantime I went to the park and saw her sitting on the bench.
I had the guts to say *I love you* and went away.

**William Zeno (11)**
Stanhope Primary School, Greenford

# Embarrassing Me

Everyone gets embarrassed at least once in their lifetime.
One time I remembered,
I split my trousers while I was acting like a boss (kind of)
I said I could shoot a hoop and slam dunk the ball which I couldn't.
I was nine and I barely knew my eight times table but luckily I learnt it.

**Hano Karem (10)**
Stanhope Primary School, Greenford

# Sadness

Everyone gets sad once in their whole life.
I remember when sometimes people didn't like me and thought I was bad at football.
For the test before, I got nought out of ten on my spelling test.
In maths I got one wrong and Shiv got all of them right.
At lunchtime I had to stay in class.
Once people nutmegged me every time in football.
Some people don't appreciate me when I do things for them.

**Kamil Sajdak (10)**
Stanhope Primary School, Greenford

# Loneliness

All my friends are running away from me.
I'm all alone and being left out.
My heart is tearing and I'm falling apart.

My friends mean so much but they don't even look.
My friends are great but they don't know.
They used to care but now they are rude.

My heart is thumping as bullets run down my face.
I get dirty looks as I'm ever so lonely.
They always say that they don't like me but I only want them more.
Now I don't have any friends and I'm all alone.
I sit at a table so lost in loneliness they don't even see me.
I'm purely lost and lonely.

**Francesca Rispin (10)**
Stanhope Primary School, Greenford

# Nervousness

I remember the day when I got to sing to the whole school in the choir,
The day I met my mum's friends at Westfield Shopping Centre.
When I came to London and Stanhope Primary School.
I sometimes get scared when doing a test,
Going to other places scares me and I get frightened.
Tears coming out of my eyes, I'm sweating bullets like it's raining.
I hope I'm never nervous again.

**Shiv Patel (10)**
Stanhope Primary School, Greenford

# Happiness!

Coming to school makes me feel like I'm a part of my class, also it brings me happiness!
Something that also makes me happy is playing my guitar.
Sharing my ideas with my friends is fun.
It gives me a chance to say how I'm feeling.
I love to play with my cousins and my siblings: *Happy times.*
Also last but not least I like making a laugh with my teacher Mr Feldman; amazing jokes.
He's a joker.
Happiness, that is my emotion.
That's how I feel about happiness.
At home, at school, also outside.

**Ashik Rasool Ansari (10)**
Stanhope Primary School, Greenford

# Love

I feel loved because I get to play with my friend.
Also I feel loved when my best friend comes to my birthday.
We always watch each other's back if we are in trouble.

When we get into fights we know that we don't mean it.
And in the end we always say sorry.
That's why it makes me feel loved.

**Ope Davies (10)**
Stanhope Primary School, Greenford

# Angry

**A** bull bursting through buildings
**N** ow no bulls attacking farms.
**G** orillas going around eating bananas.
**R** olling on the street like no one sees me.
**Y** elling with steam coming out of my nose.

**Kajus Amalevicius (8)**
Stanhope Primary School, Greenford

# Anger

**A** lways feeling glum in the sun.
**N** ot my time to be happy.
**G** oing to the boiling, beautiful beach so angry, why take me?
**E** ven smoke steaming out of my nose like a snoring bear.
**R** unning through the magnificent sea I'm still angry, what will fix me?

**Amani  (8)**
Stanhope Primary School, Greenford

# Anger

Anger and flames make me rough and tough.
The words that you tell me confuse me so much,
So I bang my head on the stairs and talk to my mind.

I try to control my anger but I just can't because it's too powerful to stop.
When I get angry orange bright flames come out of my big head.
So that means I'm very angry.
But if fire isn't on my head that means I'm not.

When my mum gives me jobs,
I get steamingly furious.
When no one plays with me I get very mad and steam pours out.

**Krish Sehmi (8)**
Stanhope Primary School, Greenford

# Bursting

**B** ursting with anger like a volcano.
**U** ndo the password for anger.
**R** oaring as loud as a lion.
**S** uddenly calming down.
**T** oday if you're angry calm yourself down.
**I** hate being angry.
**N** obody will calm me down.
**G** oing to a friend's place and trying to be happy and the only way
to be happy is to have fun.

**Ibraheem Ramzan (8)**
Stanhope Primary School, Greenford

# Happy

**H** appy as the huge rainbow shining through me.
**A** s proud as if I'm the king
**P** olite as the government letting me be the minister.
**P** oliteness running through my heart.
**Y** our happiness will get better.

**H** appy as a rabbit bouncing around.
**A** ll people watching me on stage.
**P** oliteness will make people happy.
**P** olite because God made me king.
**Y** our life will become better and happier.

**Amar Alwy (9)**
Stanhope Primary School, Greenford

# Christmas

**C** elebrate with turkey
**H** ealthy, not healthy eating too much.
**R** ice and plantain so yum.
**I** t's fun playing with crackers.
**S** unny everywhere Christmas, Christmas
**T** ime has come, I wonder what's inside, I wish I knew.
**M** um and Dad are curious to know what we got for them.
**A** t night we pray to God.
**S** unset, all in bed.

**Leanna Mensah (8)**
Stanhope Primary School, Greenford

# Happiness

Happiness is the key to success,
You'll be the best at everything.
Defeats anger every time.
Everyone loves happiness.
Happiness is the best
Because everyone is my friend.

Everyone likes me when I'm happy
I play tag like puppies running around
Oh happiness you make me new friends
Happiness flows through the school.

I'm the happiest in the school
Happiness runs around my body.
Happiness is like a speeding bullet.
Happiness lives in the happiest, healthiest places.
Where gummy bunnies and unicorns live.

**Kishal Chhetri (9)**
Stanhope Primary School, Greenford

# Happiness

Happiness follows wherever you go
Happy as a friend.
They smile wherever you go
Friends are everywhere.

Playing with friends is so much fun
Running around in the sun
Having friends like hearts
Just as sweet as strawberry tarts.

Getting ice cream after school is so happy
Especially with your friends
Always be happy as a butterfly.

**Sumedha Suntharalingum (8)**
Stanhope Primary School, Greenford

# What Do I Do?

H orses come to my house on Monday.
A mani comes to me on Tuesday and makes me laugh like a baby.
P eople love to play with me on Wednesday and scream at my toys.
P acket of crisps I eat on a Thursday.
Y o-yo I play on Friday, Saturday and Sunday!

**Fatimah Shah (8)**
Stanhope Primary School, Greenford

# Anger

I stamp my feet and shout out at my brother.
I feel like I'm melting like real snow
And my brother thinks that I'm a dripping man like rain.
My face gets red and I start to shout out.
My heart beats like a rabbit's
My heart starts to beat faster than before.
I start to run around to get him.
And I stamp my feet again.
I think this anger will never go away.
But I think it's bull.
I feel like I'm going to explode.
My fear is still red.
I want to be powerful.
But so does my brother.
And I want to get him.
But he's too fast.

**Ferdous Siddiqui (9)**
Stanhope Primary School, Greenford

# Fear/Happy/Angry

I was as angry as a furious dragon,
My legs were red and my heart was beating like a vibration of a car.
I stamped my feet and screamed.
My friend said that I was a big bully because I pushed them all.
It wasn't that fun so I calmed myself down.
And I thought what I'd done to my poor friends.
On the next day I was scared because I saw a ghost, it was scary.
But not that scary, but then I was happy
Because my little brother played a trick on me.
It was very funny.

**Samuel Kumi (8)**
Stanhope Primary School, Greenford

# Haunting Anger

Anger is bad
It also makes me feel mad.
Screeching like a scary Dracula.
Like a bullet full of anger hit me.
My huff never ends especially when people are bullying me.

The anger monsters are really dangerous.
They hate joyful songs
And the sunshine one is the worst.
It goes, 'Come on everybody smile, smile, smile,
Fill your heart with sunshine, sunshine, sunshine.'

Anger, anger raging at me.
The people will pay like I'm the volcano today.
They'll beg for mercy
And I will make them pay.

**Dillon Sivaanpu (8)**
Stanhope Primary School, Greenford

# Fear

My hands are rattling like a rattlesnake.
I am frozen on the spot.
My head is banging on the wall.
My heart is pounding like a cheetah.
Do I have to feel this way when I feel fear?
Wait a minute . . . I'm going to burst with tears.
My sweat drips like tears running from my cheeks.
Sometimes I feel like my skin is peeling off.
My mind whirls all around like I have a hurricane in my head, *boom,
whoosh!*
My fear never ends.
My eyes suddenly close.
Why do I have to feel this way, when I feel fear?

**Nivethika Gnanaseelan (8)**
Stanhope Primary School, Greenford

# My Birthday

**B** rilliant, my birthday is coming.
**I** need to think about a surprise!
**R** iding my bike is the best thing I can do!
**T** his year I'm gonna get the best surprise!
**H** o, ho, ho! Santa comes to me on my birthday.
**D** ad's gonna buy me a new Xbox One or 360.
**A** re you angry? I'm not, it's my birthday
**Y** ou want to come to my birthday?

**Jakub Tomaszewski (8)**
Stanhope Primary School, Greenford

# The Boy That Was Full Of Fear

I was full of fear, it was a man chasing me.
It was a scary night, it was not bright.
I thought I was gonna die.
I was shrieking like frozen ice.
I was like a guy.
My heart was as fast as the fastest car in the world.
Finally I got out of trouble now!

**Zakaria Amin (8)**
Stanhope Primary School, Greenford

# It's Christmas

C hristmas is fun, Christmas is happy,
H appy Christmas everyone
R inging bells and people singing carols.
I s Santa coming?
S now is fun, snow is cold.
T en presents, hip hip hooray.
M ornings are sunny and after it's snowy.
A nd Christmas pudding
S anta's beard, Santa's greedy because he likes Christmas pudding.

**Karina Patel (8)**
Stanhope Primary School, Greenford

# Christmas!

C hristmas is great,
H appy New Year.
R ight Christmas is great,
I 'm very happy that it is Christmas,
S anta will come to give us a prize.
T he presents are here,
M any happy New Years.
A nd very nice presents,
S o many presents.

**Izabella Dumitrescu (8)**
Stanhope Primary School, Greenford

# Shock!

*Surprise!*
Gosh I'm shocked!
*Wow . . . amazing!*
I'm as shocked as an electric man.
*Shock!*
My alarm bell yelled at me this morning.
Tired . . . sleepy . . .
I'm as tired as a cloud.
*Shock!*
My friends hurt me yesterday.
*Ouch! It hurts. Ouch!*
I feel the pain
*Shock!*
*All these things . . . make me . . . shocked!*

**Alex Norsworthy (8)**
Stanhope Primary School, Greenford

# Happiness And Joy

I can feel happiness, I can feel joy.
Happiness is about getting along and having fun.
Joy is about respect and sharing.
I love sharing.
Happiness tastes like ice cream,
And Joy smells like hot chocolate
And it looks like friends are for caring and sharing.
Happiness looks like a smile.
But Joy looks exciting, it sounds like laughing.
I love Happiness and Joy.

**Rohail Sheikh (8)**
Stanhope Primary School, Greenford

# Anger!

I have a lot of anger in me and it has to get out of me,
I am always frustrated, my mum always makes me go to bed,
Even though I am not tired.
I play games in bed even though I am not tired.
I broke my mum's golden jar, and she was mad.
I went to bed at five o'clock because I broke her jar.

**Jaden Awoa (8)**
Stanhope Primary School, Greenford

# Anger

Anger lives in the deep place of your body
In a cage with all of your nightmares, monsters and your greatest
fears . . .
But Anger is the scariest one of all
Because his ears have smoke coming out and he's red-faced.

To get rid of him is to take a massive breath before he takes you over.
Sometimes I scare my brothers.
I normally grind my teeth like Freddy Krueger or Freddy Fazbear.
Inside your body is a dice, roll it and pay the price if it's anger.

So don't get angry with your brothers,
Instead just take a nice breath in and out.
So never unleash the evil smile and be nice instead.
On Sunday I got angry because my brother Liam annoyed me
And I took a deep breath and said, 'I was going to attack you!'
Anger makes me shiver and quiver and shake and quake.
I can't say the word 'Anger' or I feel like I will faint or maybe die if I say
anger.

**Kieran Donovan (7)**
The Smallberry Green Primary School, Isleworth

# Oh Anger

Anger, Anger leave me alone
Why don't you have an ice cream cone?
You fierce ferocious animal go away
Never come back any day.

Oh Anger you make my face go red,
Until I actually go to bed!
Oh Anger, you massive rage
It's like a lion in a metal cage.

Big bold Anger, you're like a vile, vicious dog
You never allow me to jump for joy like a frog
When I lost the important school race
I felt like I'd melted into an embarrassing place.

When my rude, revolting sister makes me sad.
She knows I'm going to do something very bad.
Oh Anger, you don't even let me sleep
Go away you little creep.

**Laksh Khanna (8)**
The Smallberry Green Primary School, Isleworth

# The Brave Knight

One day there lived a brave knight,
Who never fought one day or one night.

One day there lived a crazy dragon,
Who always ate a cart or a wagon.

Sadly the dragon, ate the knight,
But what he remembered, was that he got into a fight.

But the town always knew that he was brave.
So they made a statue of him and put him in a grave.

And every feeling he had was mostly brave.
But the village was mad but some were still sad.

**Savir Singh Sura (8)**
The Smallberry Green Primary School, Isleworth

# Braveness, Where Are You?

Braveness, oh Braveness,
Where are you?
Up to my head,
Down to my shoe.

Tumbling in meadows,
Up in trees,
Braveness, oh Braveness,
Where are you?

Flying in the sky,
Under the ground,
Braveness, oh Braveness
Here you are.

In my hands,
Sleeping around,
By half-past two,
Which is always true.

**Dev Sinha (9)**
The Smallberry Green Primary School, Isleworth

# The Boy Who Is So Silly

There is a boy who is silly.
His name is Bailey not Billy.
He can't help laughing but he mostly giggles.
He laughs, he giggles and he wiggles.

**Bailey Nagle  (8)**
The Smallberry Green Primary School, Isleworth

# Anger Came Back

Anger came back with his red hat,
He treated me like a bat,
All the other emotions were sad,
They ran away because Anger made them mad.

Anger gets mad if you call him names,
He will burst like a volcano,
He will burst into flames.
Life will never be the same.

**Pramita Malla (8)**
The Smallberry Green Primary School, Isleworth

# Want To Eat

When I have a greedy mouth
All the food is right out
I just want to cry, cry, cry.
But I just want a few French fries.

When I am so greedy
And my mum gets very sneezy.
I have to make all the food
So my parents don't get rude.

**Pragun Pawar (8)**
The Smallberry Green Primary School, Isleworth

# Anger

Anger, Anger are you angry?
Yes, yes I am just like a big, bad bear.
Oh please don't burst like fireworks
Oh please, please, oh maybe I won't.
Oh Anger, please forgive me.
I just wanted to touch your lovely clip.

Anger, Anger don't get angry,
Because I can see that smoke is coming out of your ears.
Just like a puffing steam train.
Oh Anger, ever so angry,
I can feel that you're as hot as a boiling kettle.

Anger, Anger your hair is so beautiful,
But it is all straight. Are you angry?
Yes, yes of course I am.
Aren't I always like this, can you tell me?
Oh Anger, your skin is so spiky, are you sweaty?

Come, come on Anger, just calm down,
All you have to do is take a deep breath.
Don't, don't shout like a gust of wind Anger.
Or I will do that to you.
OK, OK I'll try not to or maybe . . . oh no you don't. Oh fine!

Anger, Anger, can I ask you a question?
Yes, but a quick one.
OK, oh also a ten second one.
Why do you always grit your teeth like a falling pencil?
Because I'm angry can't you see?
Oh I thought that was going to be the answer.

**Amelia Rosinska (7)**
The Smallberry Green Primary School, Isleworth

# Love

One day I was staring at the one I liked.
Happy thoughts went into my head,
Being the one who's in love,
I was blushing like a pool of blinking eyes.

Love is when you stare at somebody who is handsome.
Love is beautiful,
Love is care. Love is amazing. Love looks after you.
Everybody has the right to love someone even though you are poor.
Love can make you cry when you kiss your true love.

Love is for everybody not just for you.
Everybody shares love with their boy friends and girl friends.
Not just their families.
But they need enough love to share with their children.
Everybody has enough love for their family.
Love gives harmony. Love gives help. Love gives care.

**Nikitha Vegesna (7)**
The Smallberry Green Primary School, Isleworth

# The Last Life Of Mine

All dead, all gone, the only one.
Who is done? I had enough of sitting in mud and digging in the trench.
Deep, deep in my heart I feel lonely and nearly dead.
Deadly poison is going through my body.
I feel done and I am gone, I am in Heaven.
And I have the rest now to do, my own nest to leave.
I am going to start a new adventure
Goodbye . . .

**Hatem Sharif-Younis (9)**
The Smallberry Green Primary School, Isleworth

# Hunger

When you are hungry you cry,
When you are hungry you feel numb and dumb.
To get food, you will try and try and try.
It will take over you.
And you will jump and stumble,
And you will always mumble,
Your day will be done for custard and some crumble.

When you are given food you shout, 'Calloo, callay!'
And this time,
It will definitely make your day.

The feeling will bite you.
And you will slowly fall away,
But it will always keep you away
From the crisps and burgers.
That do not make your day!

**Ansh Deepak (9)**
The Smallberry Green Primary School, Isleworth

# Sadness

My tummy was hurting, my nose was red
I struggled vigorously in my uncomfortable bed.
Everywhere I go, everywhere I see,
Lots of people laughing at me.
My face was blue as the sky, sad as can be,
I wish that they could see me.
Tears flowing down like raindrops in the blue sky.
And all the moments all going by.
Water splashing down my cheeks
And flowing down for many weeks.

**Eesha Babbra (9)**
The Smallberry Green Primary School, Isleworth

# Joy

I had a dream,
While I was eating ice cream
Feeling joy said a little boy.
It is really fun,
When I'm not numb!

**Ellie Louise Simpson (10)**
The Smallberry Green Primary School, Isleworth

# Joy

When I had a dream,
I had an ice cream.

It was of joy,
Said the little boy.

It was good,
When candy was chewed.

It was eight,
And everything was great.

I said goodbye,
And they replied.

**Maral Gan-Och (10)**
The Smallberry Green Primary School, Isleworth

# Happiness

Happy, happy, happy, you're always expressed with joy.
This is what makes me a happy boy
I want to shout out loud like a pirate shouting, 'Ahoy!'

Joy, joy, joy, he always wants to come out and play.
He always gives and pays every day.
He comes out in May
Because it is his favourite year,
He never has a tear.

**Amaran Shaan Bansal (9)**
The Smallberry Green Primary School, Isleworth

# Sadness, Sadness, Sadness

Sadness, oh sadness, why do you come?
The room full of tears
Sometimes you make me feel numb.
Inside me it's full of fear.

**Zainab Shiekh (9)**
The Smallberry Green Primary School, Isleworth

# Hello Joy

'Hi, I'm Joy, nice to meet you.'
She seems very pleased to meet you.
'Nothing in this world ever goes wrong.'
'Frown, enraged, infuriated, fuming?'
'What on earth do they mean?'
Joy often yells to me.
'Delight love it, Sadness despises it.'
She repeats day after day
Joy and I are now the best of friends.

**Yasmin Warsame (9)**
The Smallberry Green Primary School, Isleworth

# Fear, Fear, Fear!

Fear, Fear go away
You are coming at me like
A lion in a cage.
Hate always comes from
Your way which is
Always in the deepest, darkest place.
Nobody likes him,
Everybody is scared of him.
He never comes out in May
Because of all the sunny days.

**Dennis Kelmendi (9)**
The Smallberry Green Primary School, Isleworth

# Sunshine And Roses

Sadness lives in the coldest places.
Where the tears and water flows.
Sometimes he bursts out with tears.
Being left out makes all the days go dark and blue.
The most annoying emotion all around.
The only thing that can stop him is sunshine and roses.

**Grace Marie Ellis (9)**
The Smallberry Green Primary School, Isleworth

# Abdullah's Fear

Fear and Anger is the worst thing in my life.
I thought someone just tapped me on the back.
I got scared and I didn't know what to do.
Fear, Fear please go away from my head.
I got so angry that I couldn't do anything.
Why does this happen to me?
It's like a monster wants to kidnap me in a cage.
So Fear, Fear get out of my head.
I'm in a haunted house and I don't know who brought me here.
I will take a deep breath and get my anger
And my fear away from my head.
I hope I don't have these in my dreams.
It's like Anger will eat me alive and someone wants to hide.

**Abdullah Ahsan Dar (10)**
The Smallberry Green Primary School, Isleworth

# Annoying, Annoying

You always make me angry.
You always make me frustrated.
If you come back again we will catch you.
Annoying is the worst emotion if it can't do something.
He will get angry, will not come back until he has calmed down.

**Anu Sudhagar (9)**
The Smallberry Green Primary School, Isleworth

# Happiness

I felt happy when I got a new coat,
And went on a boat,
I caught a fish,
And cooked it in a dish.
I play with my cat.
And put him in a hat.

**Oscar Connor (9)**
The Smallberry Green Primary School, Isleworth

[]

# Happy

Happy feeling just for you.
Happy dream ready for you.
Outside playing cheerfully,
Just like you,
Teachers ready to teach
Let's learn together: One . . . two . . . three.
The bell ringing, *ding, ding, ding!*
Let's say goodbye to all your friends . . .

**Maryam Ahmed (10)**
The Smallberry Green Primary School, Isleworth

# Anger's The Worst Feeling

Oh, the worst feeling is here. It's coming for me.
I'm so scared, I feel like my heart is going to get torn.
I want to fight the feeling but it's getting the better of me,
With all this fighting, I seem like a busy bee.
As the anger alarm sounds, I will win my confidence back.
Anger, his face goes red with envy,
As would anybody's face if they were in the same situation.

**Faisal Abdi (10)**
The Smallberry Green Primary School, Isleworth

# Fearing The New Future

Mum and Dad are really mad,
Angry as can be.
Fearing what future could happen
Run away and be free
Hide and slide.
Welcome to the new pride.
How's the new life
Daydreaming and daydreaming
Still shouting at me.
Run away, run away
Fear is in my head.
Fear is like a creepy-crawly
Tickling in my head.

**Maryam Khatun (9)**
The Smallberry Green Primary School, Isleworth

# Bashful Birthday

My bashful birthday was colourful and fun,
When I saw the cake I started to run,
'It is full of cream,' I said
As I started to push my way through the crowd.

My exciting birthday was super cool,
Especially when I saw the pool,
When I got out there were drinks,
When I drank it, slippery slipped.

My fun birthday was super big
Even when I saw the chick,
It was yellow and furry, it had four legs,
But no hands, it was cute but not fun.

**Aya Jaff (8)**
The Smallberry Green Primary School, Isleworth

# Happiness

Happy like a clown
Jumping up and down on my bed.

Chatter, chatter, I can't stop chatting
Chatter, I blast into space.

Sing, sing like a bird on a tree.
I'm feeling so happy, I feel like I'm going to burst.

*Pop, pop!* I feel hot
Hyper, hyper like a bomb.

When I stop I start to be a chatterbox
Then I burst into flames for a good reason.

I am OK, I say but I'm hyper like a mad joey.

**Joseph Wimalasekera (8)**
The Smallberry Green Primary School, Isleworth

# Blood Brother!

When my brother teases me I go wild;
As a wolf from the west,
He is as big as a bear.
Frightening as a fire and as fiery as a fox.
And creepy as a creaking clock.
He likes to battle but there's no rattle.

**Abdikadir Mohamed Ahmed (8)**
The Smallberry Green Primary School, Isleworth

POETRY EMOTIONS - Middlesex

# Anger

Anger, Anger, big and strong
Bubbling like a kettle, lashing about
As hot as fire, as red as red as blood
He's aggressive, he's mad, he's very, very bad

Anger, Anger, big and strong
He's getting badder, he'll make the children sadder
At the end of the week he'll make a cloud of shame
So he can make the game

Anger, Anger, big and strong
Tensing up his fist, punching everyone
He's like a nightmare night and he's as angry as a monster
He's always on the run, to fight you with a gun

Anger, Anger, big and strong
He's as hot as a steam train
Dripping like a tap his heart is jumping with cruelty
Because all he knows is angry, angry, angry

Anger, Anger, big and strong
He'll make pots clash and glass smash
Anger, Anger please calm down
You'll only make things worse
If you do this stuff it's just too much

With a warm little breeze Anger goes away
Whenever you are angry just take a deep breath.

**Aisha Chew (7)**
The Smallberry Green Primary School, Isleworth

# Sadness

Sadness lives in the coldest places where all the deep things come
out.
My face droops and my eyes close.
Cold tears drip down my face.
Luckily I'm sad but not bad.
I walk as slow as a turtle, I say bye and start to cry.

My hairs stand on end
And it's like they are going to bend like a bear breaking bark.
My body starts to shiver like I'm getting bigger.
I stand under a cloud of shame and never play a game.

**Darnell Judd (7)**
The Smallberry Green Primary School, Isleworth

# Sadness

I was sad because someone was mad.
My tears were like rain dripping from the sky.
My throat was dry, it was like I was going to die.
I was sadder than a clown in thunder.
Exploding with tears from a miserable thunderstorm.
Sometimes I believe rain is a giant's tear.
When I was lonely I said, 'I'm never happy when I've got no friends.'
Things that make me sad are being left out, people hurting me,
Also people saying rude things about me.

**Fearne L Cotterill (7)**
The Smallberry Green Primary School, Isleworth

# Anger

My eyes are making a pool of anger and I feel angry like a big bad bear.
I am burning like a volcano, I am ruby-red rage and my hands are sweating.
I am as red as flaming fire bursting into flames.

My legs are trembling with rage and burning purple, I feel like I am a mad white rhino.
And I am steaming just like a steam train.
My legs feel so feeble, the feeblest as can be.

My toes are aching so much just like a piece of dirt crumbling to dust.
And my feet feel very hot just like a boiling hot pot.
I am so very angry that my shoes just feel like they are about to come off.

**Posy Manthey (8)**
The Smallberry Green Primary School, Isleworth

# My Perfect Day

On my eighth birthday,
I had a lot of fun
But when the cake arrived I was having too much fun.

On my sixth Eid.
I had a lot of trouble
But when the music arrived.
I went crazy like a bride.

On my sister's birthday,
We had a lot of fun,
But she went crazy like a loose mouse.

**Rania Benzekri (8)**
The Smallberry Green Primary School, Isleworth

**111**

# Anger In My Room

When someone is mean,
I feel I will scream,
When I have a monstrous mess in my room,
It looks like there was a big boom.

When my friend is really rude,
And I don't get any food,
I just want to cry,
I eat some hot fries,
I feel so hot like a cooking pot.

I was so greedy,
I took all the creamy cake,
But now there is none in the bake
I'm now so sad and that's bad,
Because no one wants to play with me
Or come round to have some tea.

**Julia Kania (8)**
The Smallberry Green Primary School, Isleworth

# Excited

Stars at night are shining so bright in the sky like a bright shining light.
They light up the day and night.
Halloween is a nightmare to my brother and my poor mother,
Me and Dad run with joy like a little dog.
Easter is like a bunny, scratching you around the grass it's so funny.

**Ella-Paige Jones (8)**
The Smallberry Green Primary School, Isleworth

# Marvellous Memories

Happy horses like to neigh
They also like to eat hay.
Laying down in their bunk
They like Polos as a treat.
In the field under the sun,
Now their day is done.

Stars at night,
Shining so bright
In the sky up so high,
I can touch the sky.

Halloween is scary
Like a skeleton
I definitely don't scream like a newborn baby.

**Ella Georgia Jack Miles (8)**
The Smallberry Green Primary School, Isleworth

# Future Dynamite

My pet puma gives,
Me my future twirling.
In my pink sparkling
Hula-hoop.

Jumping in my pretty
Pride, feeling very bright
Like dynamite.

In my eyes, through my sight,
Skipping with my diamonds
Right beside my night light.

**Aaliyah Abdihakim Yasin (8)**
The Smallberry Green Primary School, Isleworth

# My Happy Destination

My mummy gave me a huggy as it was my birthday
She gave me a dummy to play with.
My brother gave me a mansion
But my daddy gave me a baddy.
I give more than receive,
It's just that I am happy.
I just want money to donate
But my heart is much more important than life.
Joy can spread through your life.
Remember, joy can spread through life.

**Fizan Hussain (9)**
The Smallberry Green Primary School, Isleworth

Est.1991

# Young Writers Information

We hope you have enjoyed reading this book – and that you will continue to in the coming years.

If you're a young writer who enjoys reading and creative writing, or the parent of an enthusiastic poet or story writer, do visit our website www.youngwriters.co.uk. Here you will find free competitions, workshops and games, as well as recommended reads, a poetry glossary and our blog.

If you would like to order further copies of this book, or any of our other titles, then please give us a call or visit **www.youngwriters.co.uk.**

Young Writers
Remus House
Coltsfoot Drive
Peterborough
PE2 9BF
(01733) 890066 / 898110
**info@youngwriters.co.uk**